Louisiana,
the Jewel of the Deep South

Louisiana,
the Jewel of the Deep South

By Johnette Downing • Illustrated by Julia Marshall

PELICAN PUBLISHING COMPANY

GRETNA 2015

To precious jewels, the children of Louisiana — J. D.
To my husband, Dylan, who celebrates my successes — J. M.

The word "Pelican" and the depiction of a pelican are
trademarks of Pelican Publishing Company, Inc., and are
registered in the U.S. Patent and Trademark Office.

Library of Congress Cataloging-in-Publication Data

Downing, Johnette.
  Louisiana, the jewel of the deep South / by Johnette Downing ; illustrated by Julia Marshall.
     pages cm
  Summary: "Louisiana became a state in 1812. This informative picture book introduces young readers to the state symbols, from its flag to the state vegetable. A timeline provides the year that each item was officially designated"—Provided by publisher.
  Audience: Ages 5 to 8.
  ISBN 978-1-4556-2096-8 (hardcover : alkaline paper) — ISBN 978-1-4556-2097-5 (e-book) 1. Louisiana—Juvenile literature. 2. Emblems, State—Louisiana—Juvenile literature. I. Marshall, Julia, 1989- illustrator. II. Title.
  F369.3.D68 2015
  976.3--dc23

                    2015011704

Printed in Malaysia
Published by Pelican Publishing Company, Inc.
1000 Burmaster Street, Gretna, Louisiana 70053

LOUISIANA, THE JEWEL OF THE DEEP SOUTH

Louisiana became a state in 1812.

The flag flies over Louisiana: Union, Justice, Confidence.

Brown pelican is the state bird.
Catahoula is the state dog.

Crawfish is the crustacean.
Bald cypress is the state tree.

Honeybees buzz 'round magnolias.
Black bear roam through irises.

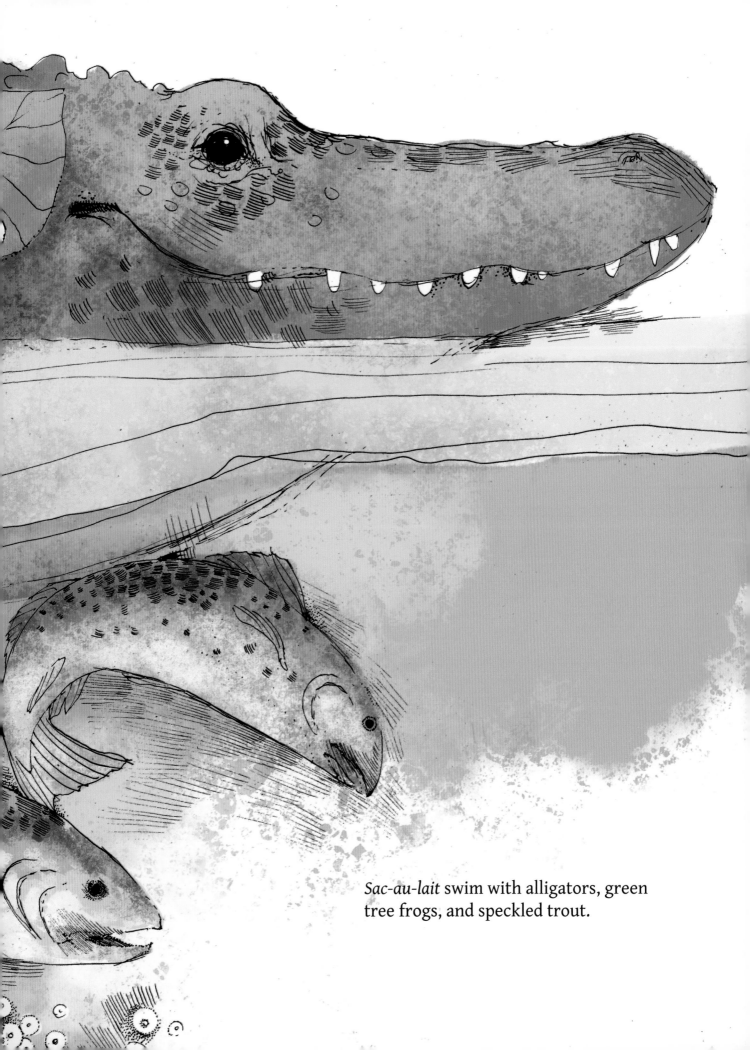

Sac-au-lait swim with alligators, green tree frogs, and speckled trout.

Blue, white, and gold are the state colors.
The fleur-de-lis is the state symbol.

Creole tomato is the vegetable plant.
Agate is the gemstone.

You'll love the food in Louisiana: gumbo and sweet beignets, sweet potatoes and strawberries, and Natchitoches meat pies.

You'll hear great music in Louisiana. Accordions play Cajun tunes. There is also Zydeco, Dixieland jazz, swamp pop, Creole, and swamp blues.

Along the rivers and in the bayous, across the prairies and the swamps, through hills and fields, and on the coastline, songs and smiles fill every house.

Come celebrate with friends and family on Fat Tuesday,
Mardi Gras. With our *joie de vivre*, we'll pass a good time.
Lassiez les bons temps rouler.

Between Texas and Mississippi, Arkansas and the Gulf of Mexico, you'll find my homeland: Louisiana, the jewel of the Deep South.

Timeline

Date	Designation	Symbol
1812	Statehood (18th State in the Union)	Louisiana
1900	Flower	Magnolia
1902	Seal	
1912	Flag	Union, Justice, Confidence
1952	March Song	"Louisiana, My Home Sweet Home," words by Sammie McKenzie and Lou Lavoy, music by Castro Carazo
1954	Day	Louisiana Day, April 30
1963	Tree	Bald Cypress
1966	Bird	Brown Pelican
1970	Song	"Give Me Louisiana," by Doralice Fontane
1972	Colors	Blue, White, and Gold

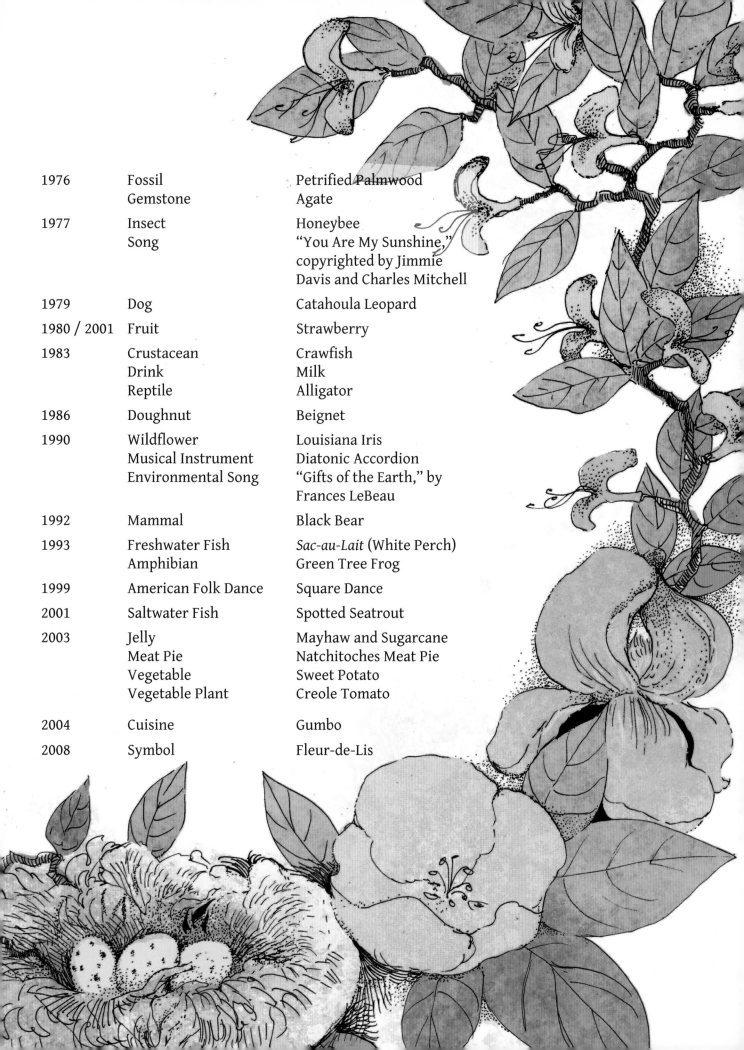

1976	Fossil	Petrified Palmwood
	Gemstone	Agate
1977	Insect	Honeybee
	Song	"You Are My Sunshine," copyrighted by Jimmie Davis and Charles Mitchell
1979	Dog	Catahoula Leopard
1980 / 2001	Fruit	Strawberry
1983	Crustacean	Crawfish
	Drink	Milk
	Reptile	Alligator
1986	Doughnut	Beignet
1990	Wildflower	Louisiana Iris
	Musical Instrument	Diatonic Accordion
	Environmental Song	"Gifts of the Earth," by Frances LeBeau
1992	Mammal	Black Bear
1993	Freshwater Fish	*Sac-au-Lait* (White Perch)
	Amphibian	Green Tree Frog
1999	American Folk Dance	Square Dance
2001	Saltwater Fish	Spotted Seatrout
2003	Jelly	Mayhaw and Sugarcane
	Meat Pie	Natchitoches Meat Pie
	Vegetable	Sweet Potato
	Vegetable Plant	Creole Tomato
2004	Cuisine	Gumbo
2008	Symbol	Fleur-de-Lis

Louisiana, the Jewel of the Deep South

Music and lyrics © 2012 Johnette Downing
Wiggle Worm Records, ASCAP